This book belongs to

_____

To request permissions, contact the publisher at pappu.sravanti@gmail.com.

Paperback ISBN: 978-0-578-25-044-1

Hardcover ISBN: 978-1-639-44-210-2

First paperback edition June 2021.

Cover art, Illustrations and Layout by Gaurav Bhatnagar

Dedication

To all kids across the world

To Mrs. Seema Kazim Ahmed, you will be missed forever

To the story-tellers of Chandamama, Tinkle, Gokulam and Champak magazines

To all my friends for their suggestions and corrections

To my parents, in-laws and family for always being there

Last but never the least, to my loving husband, without whose support this book would not have been possible. You are the best decision I've ever made.

The Unexpected Visitor

Lily and Evan's was a small and happy family. They lived with their parents in the foothills of Alaskan mountains. One snowy day, the family heard a knock on the door. It was an old man. Given the kind and generous family they were, they let him in.

"Where are you from?", the mother asked.

"I traveled all the way from India."

The children were enthralled. The world they know of only comprised their village. Excited, they circled and showered him with questions about his journey.

While mother got busy making some hot and creamy soup for the old man, he started narrating his story.

"I remember being in deep sleep. Suddenly, I visualized myself floating above my body. I have little idea how it happened. So, I took a stroll. On my way, I crossed a forest that unfortunately caught fire. All animals were running hither and tither for shelter. A baby deer was one of them. Petrified, it could not move. I stood there feeling bad for her. Gladly, her mother came to her rescue. They were oblivious to the presence of a hungry tiger, ready to attack!"

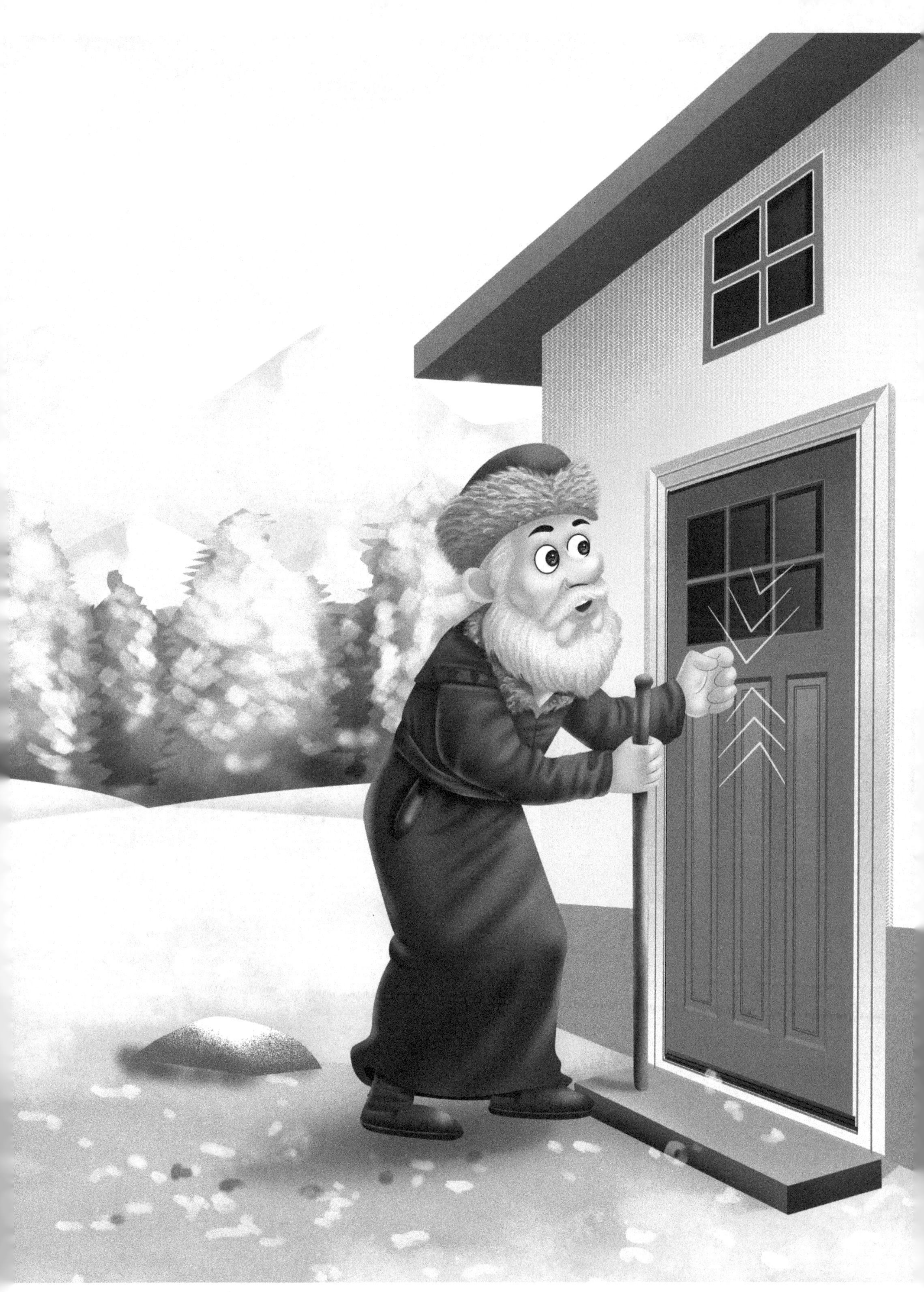

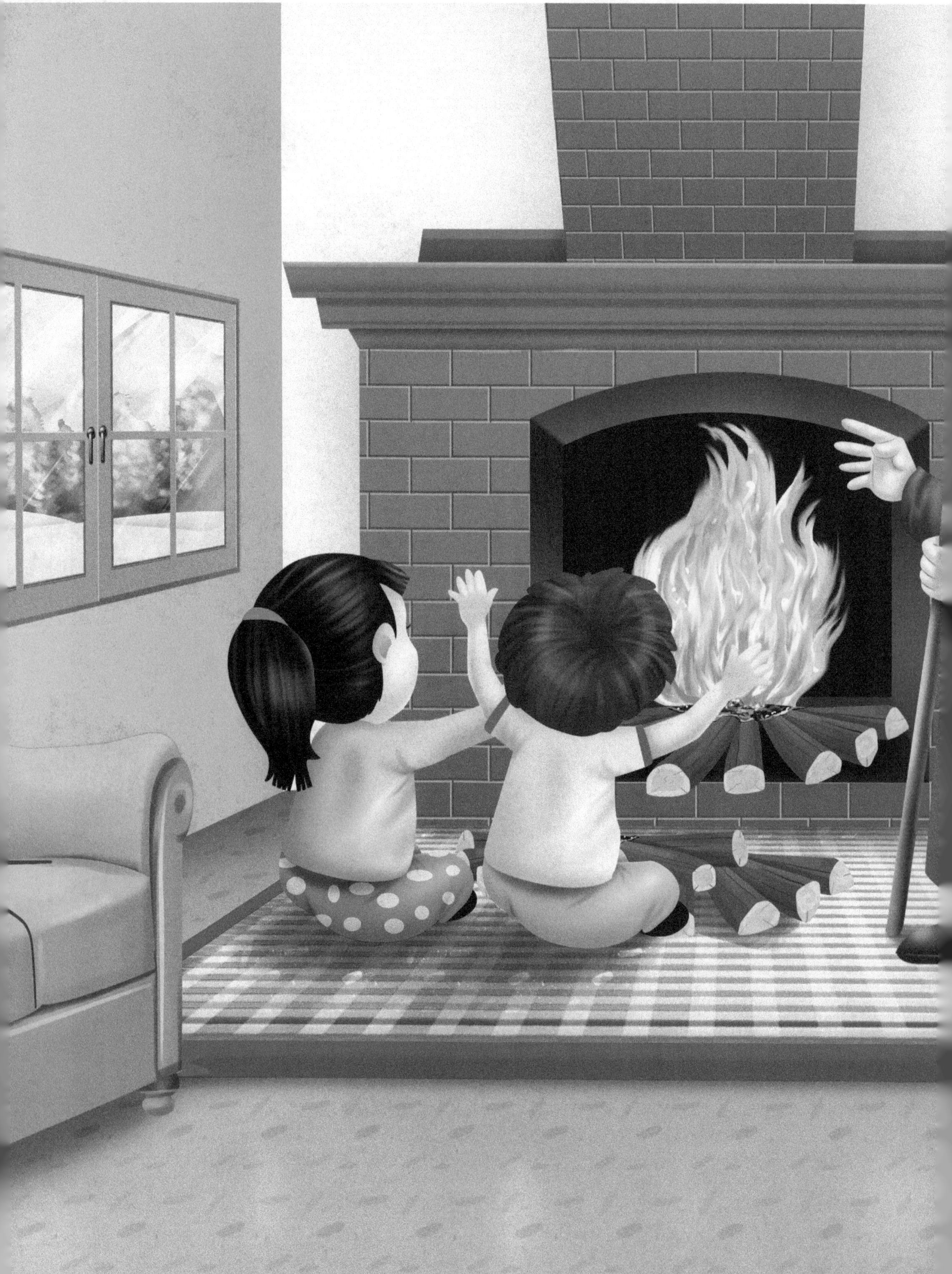

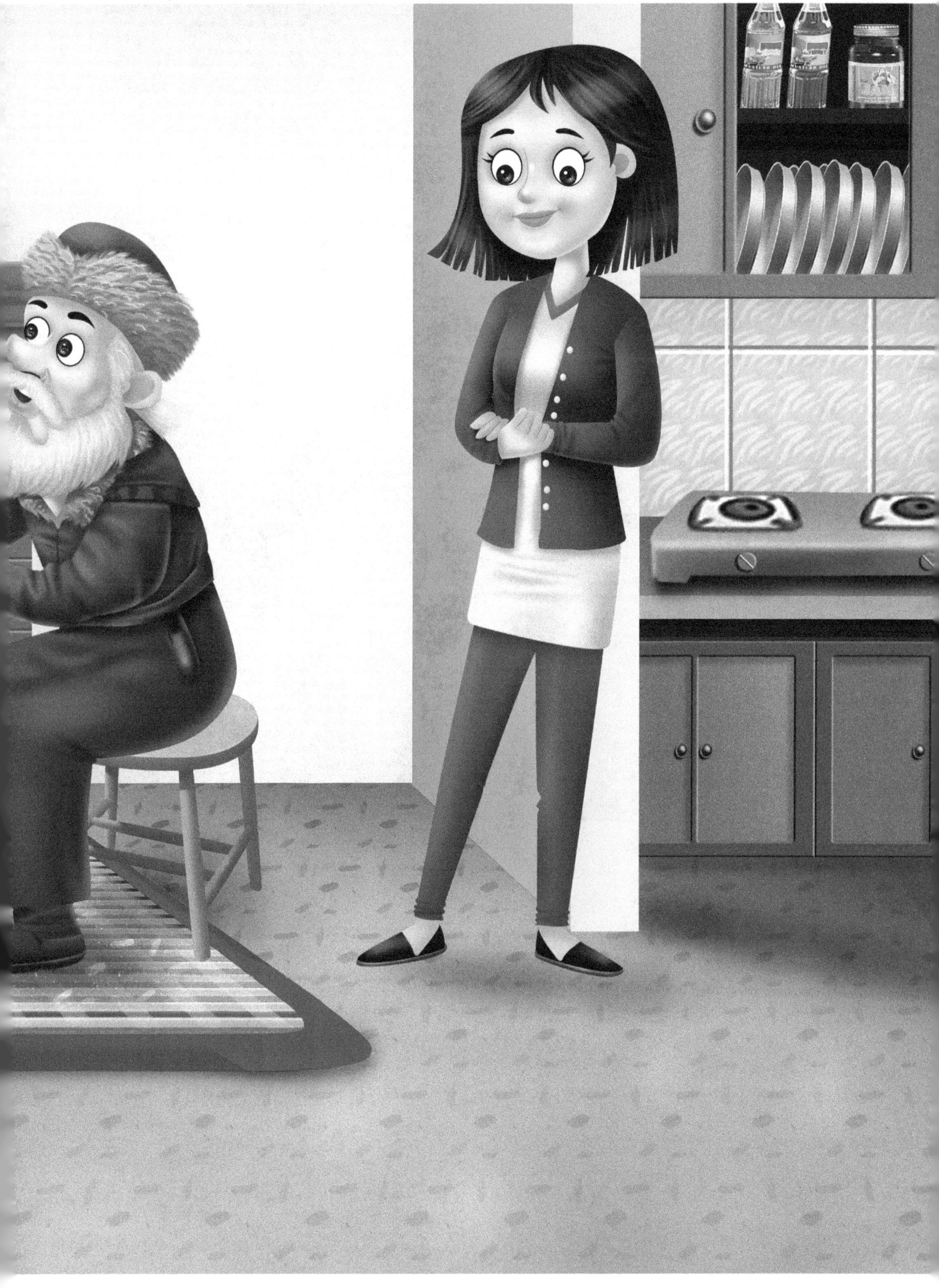

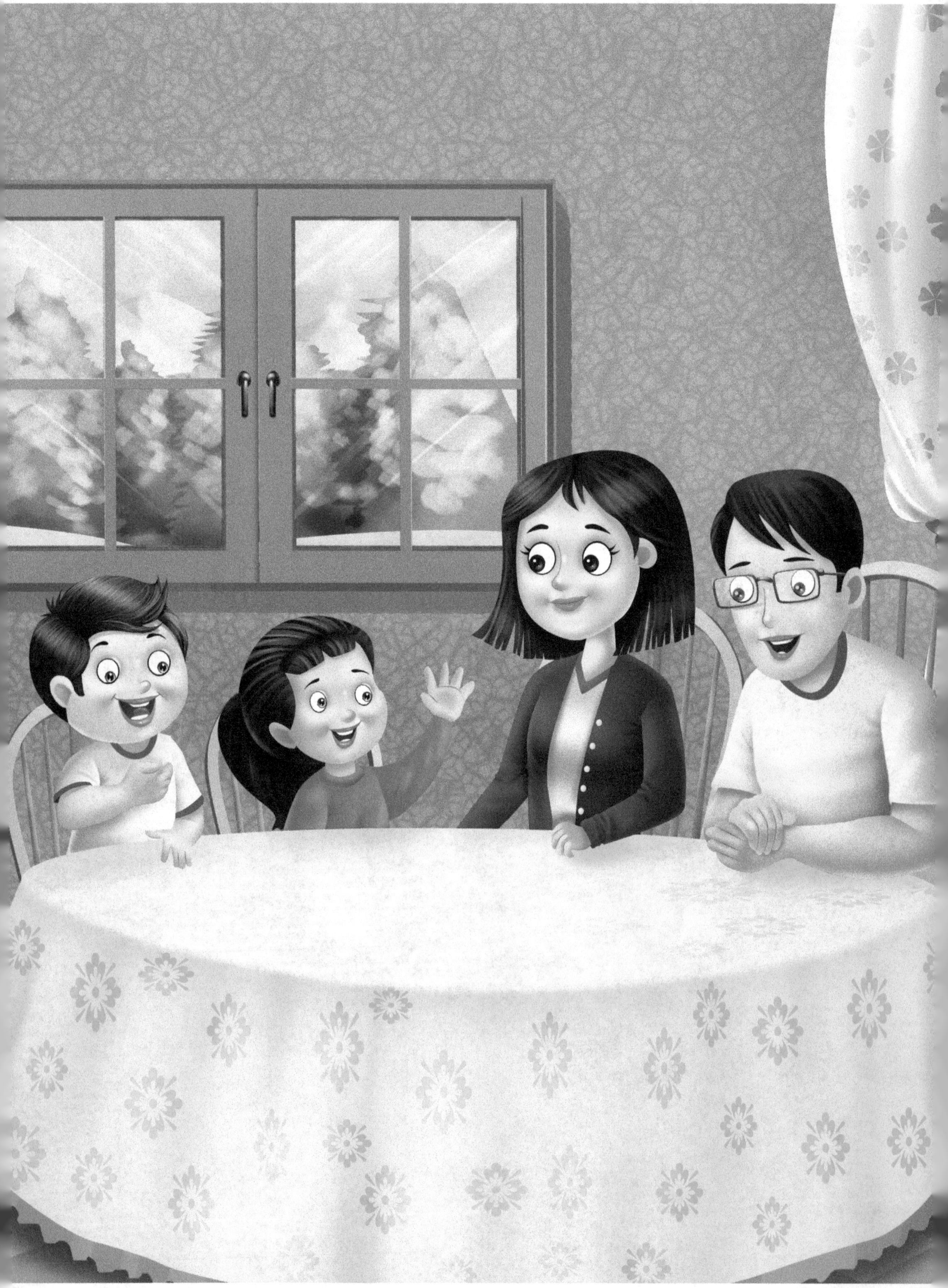

"Did the tiger attack them?", the children questioned, shocked. The old man smiled.

"No, it did not. Thankfully, a herd of elephants scared away the tiger."

The kids felt relieved to know that the baby and mommy deer were safe.

"But why didn't you try to save the baby deer?"

The old man smiled and went on.

"Now I reached a desert. The heat was scorching. A couple of camels lay by the oasis, lazily chewing on the grass. There lay a man next to them. He appeared weak and parched. He had little strength to get up. I stood there feeling bad for him. Suddenly, this bandit appeared from nowhere and tried to attack the man!" "Did the bandit rob him?" the children gasped.

"No, he did not. Luckily, a caravan that stopped to rest at the oasis spotted the bandit and the poor man. They rescued the man and offered him water."

"You could have helped, right? You could have offered him water!"

The old man smiled and went on.

"Now I am in a snow mountain valley. The view cannot be put into words. The mountains looked like inverted snow cones. Sun rays falling on the tip made it look like a cherry."

"Wow!"

"Yes, dear children. It is beauty beyond words. Anyway, as I was admiring the beauty, I overheard a loud scream. It was a huge bear chasing a woman! I could not help but feel bad for her." "Did the bear attack her?" The old man smiled.

"No, a man with a rifle happened to pass by. He noticed what was happening and managed to chase the bear away by firing bullets in the air."

"Thank god!", the children exclaimed.

"Why did you not attempt to save any of them? It is our moral responsibility to always help someone in need. Do your best, God takes care of the rest," the children uttered.

"Ah God!", smiled the old man. "Yes, God always helps those who help others."

The mother walked in with a bowl of soup in a tray.

"Sorry sir, this is all we have. It has been two days since we ate some proper food. My husband went hunting. He will be back with something for us by noon. Please stay over for lunch."

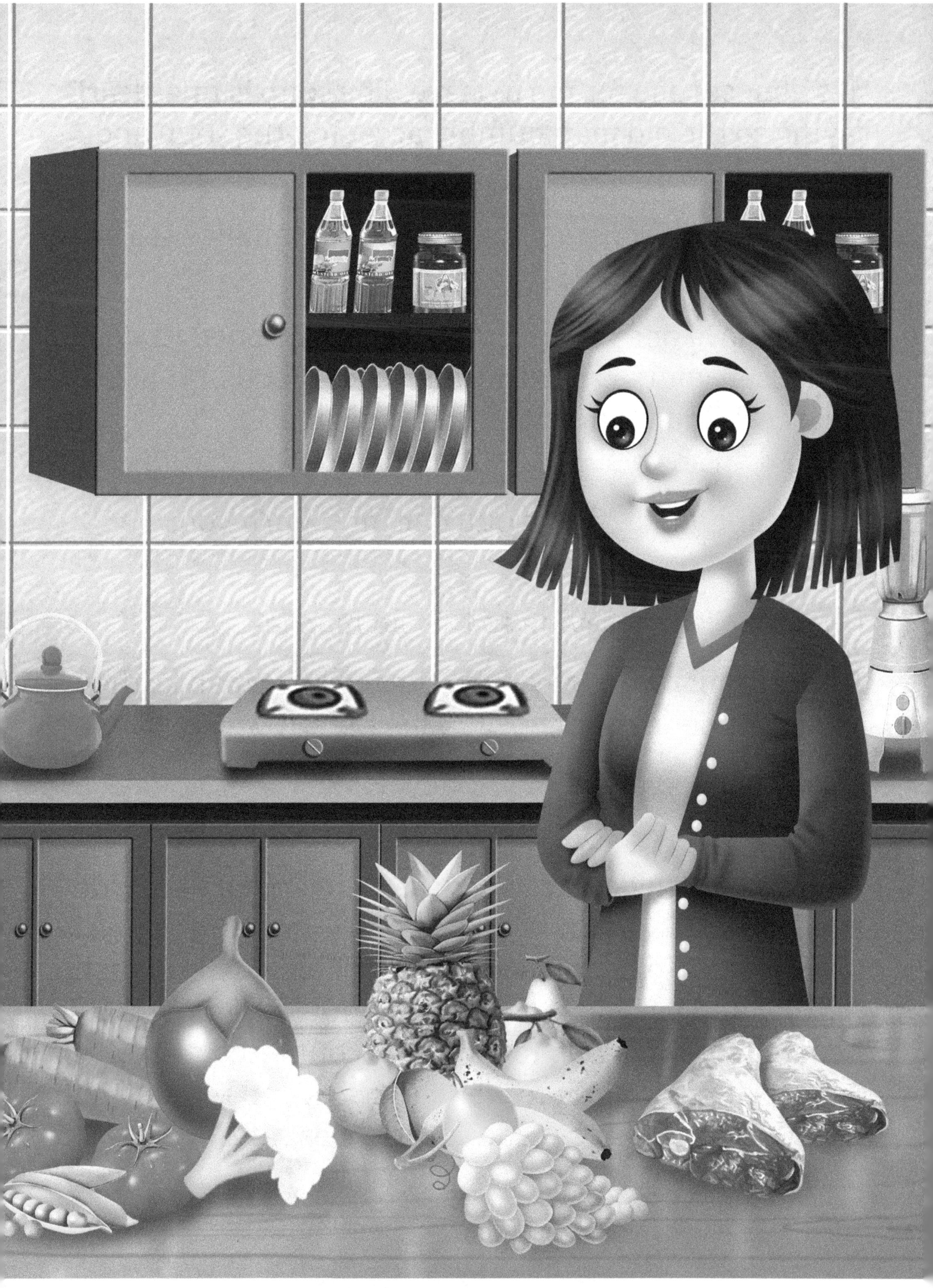

"It's almost time for me to leave. The soup is fine, dear!" saying so the old man humbly accepted the soup and finished it.

"Thank you for hosting me dear sweet family, Let's hope we meet again!"

"Wait, I have one last question. You mentioned that you visualized yourself floating above your body. So, are you real? Or a fragment of your imagination?", the kids wanted an answer.

"That's for you to figure out, darlings. With your permission,

I will take leave," saying so the old man left.

As the family wondered who the mystery man is, they heard the door knock again. This time, it was the father.

"Glad that you are home, honey! How was your day? Did you manage to get any food?", the mother asked.

"It was a rough day, dear. I chased a blacktail deer while it tried to escape. Upon following her, I noticed she was just trying to get to her baby. My heart sank when I saw the mother and baby together. I could not kill. So, I started heading for home. On my way, I encountered a man being robbed at gunpoint. I responded quick and rescued him from the robber and made sure he was safe."

"Oh my god, really", the other three exclaimed.

"That's not all! Close to home, I came across a lady being chased by a bear. I scared the bear away by firing bullets in the air." "Dad! We had guest in here earlier who told us same stories!" "A guest? Who?", the father questioned.

"Well, there was an old man here earlier, who narrated almost similar stories. It was like he was following you all the while!"

The family once again wondered who this old man was.

As the mother got back to kitchen, she was surprised to find the kitchen full of groceries and food items enough to last them the entire winter! They appeared from nowhere, like magic. She recalled the old man's words:

GOD HELPS THOSE WHO HELP OTHERS

The Gemstone Swing

"A swing!?", exclaimed the twins Sarayu and Kautilya.

It was difficult to contain their excitement. The Akondi family recently moved to a new house with huge backyard. Mr. Akondi promised the kids a swing once it is summertime. They purchased wood from a local store to build a pergola and swing. The plan was to hang the swing to pergola.

It was a tough job, especially with little help at hand. The kids invested their entire strength in helping their father. Those little helpers followed him everywhere he went. They carried tools, helped measure and cut wood, sand and paint it.

Mr. Akondi usually preferred to work in the mornings since their backyard was west facing. The kids loved their job. They worked on what they wanted and, they got paid for it! It was complete job satisfaction.

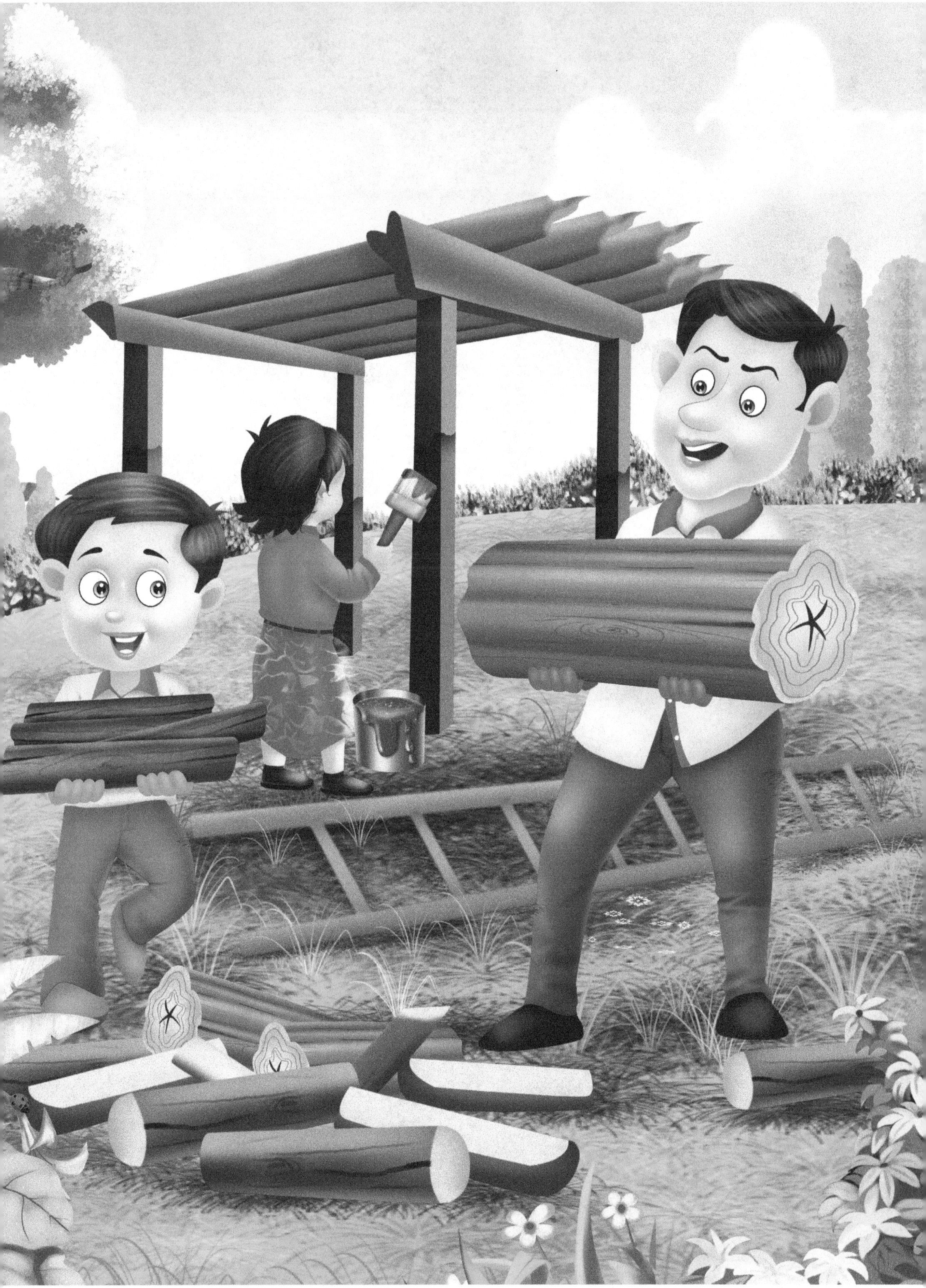

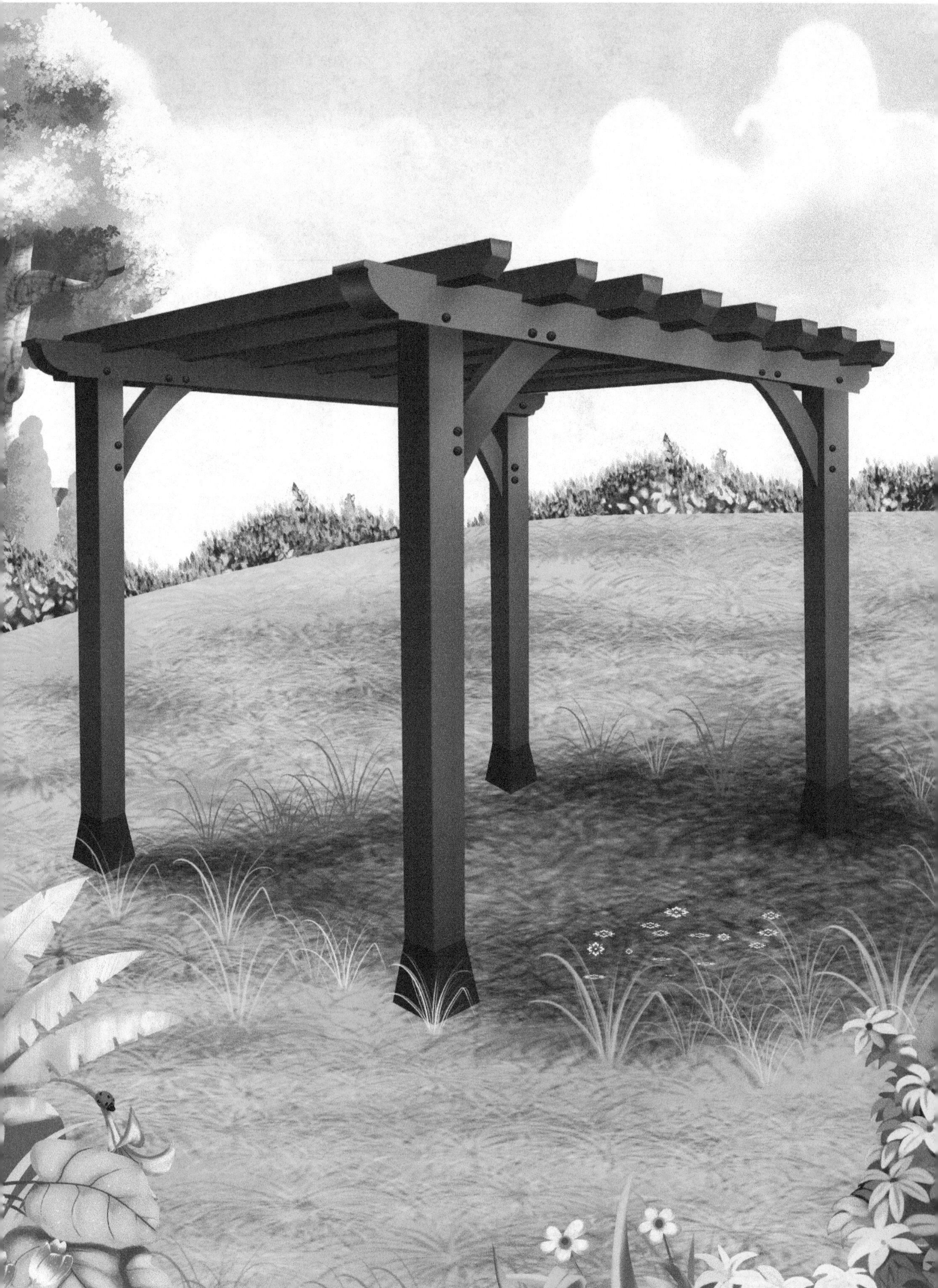

Finally, after four months of hard work, the pergola is up. As it was dusk already, Mrs. Akondi advised that they should put up the swing next day. That night, the kids had dinner and slept early. Unaware of Sarayu and Kautilya's knowledge, their parents planned on installing the swing that night as a surprise. They wanted to see their happy and surprised faces when they wake up the next morning. Mr. And Mrs. Akondi had fun time installing the swing that night.

They talked about how happy the kids would be.

Soon after they finished the installation, the entire city was hit by snowstorm caused by the Arctic outbreak.

The next morning, Sarayu and Kautilya woke up with sheer excitement. It did not last long. The snow disappointed them. They sat by the window that overlooked the pergola, admiring the swing.

The storm lasted for almost a week, with temperatures dropping below sub-zeroes. It was rough winter. Almost three months went by since the kids stepped into their backyard.

They would sit by the window every day, and plan things to do once they were allowed in the backyard.

"Let's decorate it with hanging floral pots!"

"Let's hang string lights all over the roof and multi-color lights on the swing!"

"Wow, then the swing would look like it's adorned with gemstones!"

"I feel bad for them", expressed Mrs. Akondi.

"I feel bad as well. But this is a helpless situation. I do not want them to catch cold and fall ill. Besides, patience is a virtue. Let us see how long they can wait for something they desire so bad," exclaimed Mr. Akondi.

It was April 24, Sarayu and Kautilya's birthday. The parents woke them up at midnight and brought them downstairs. For the first time in months, the backyard door opened.

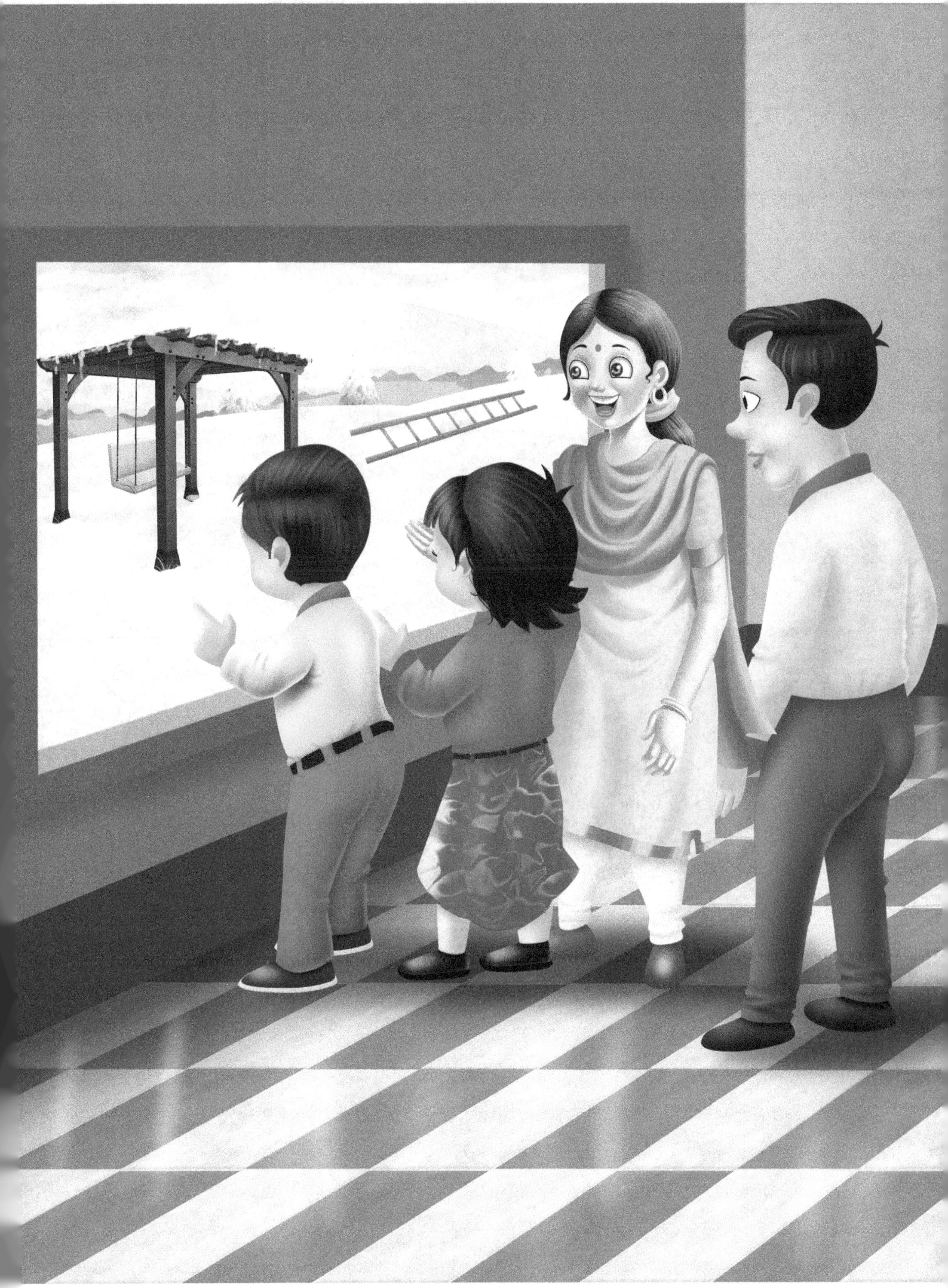

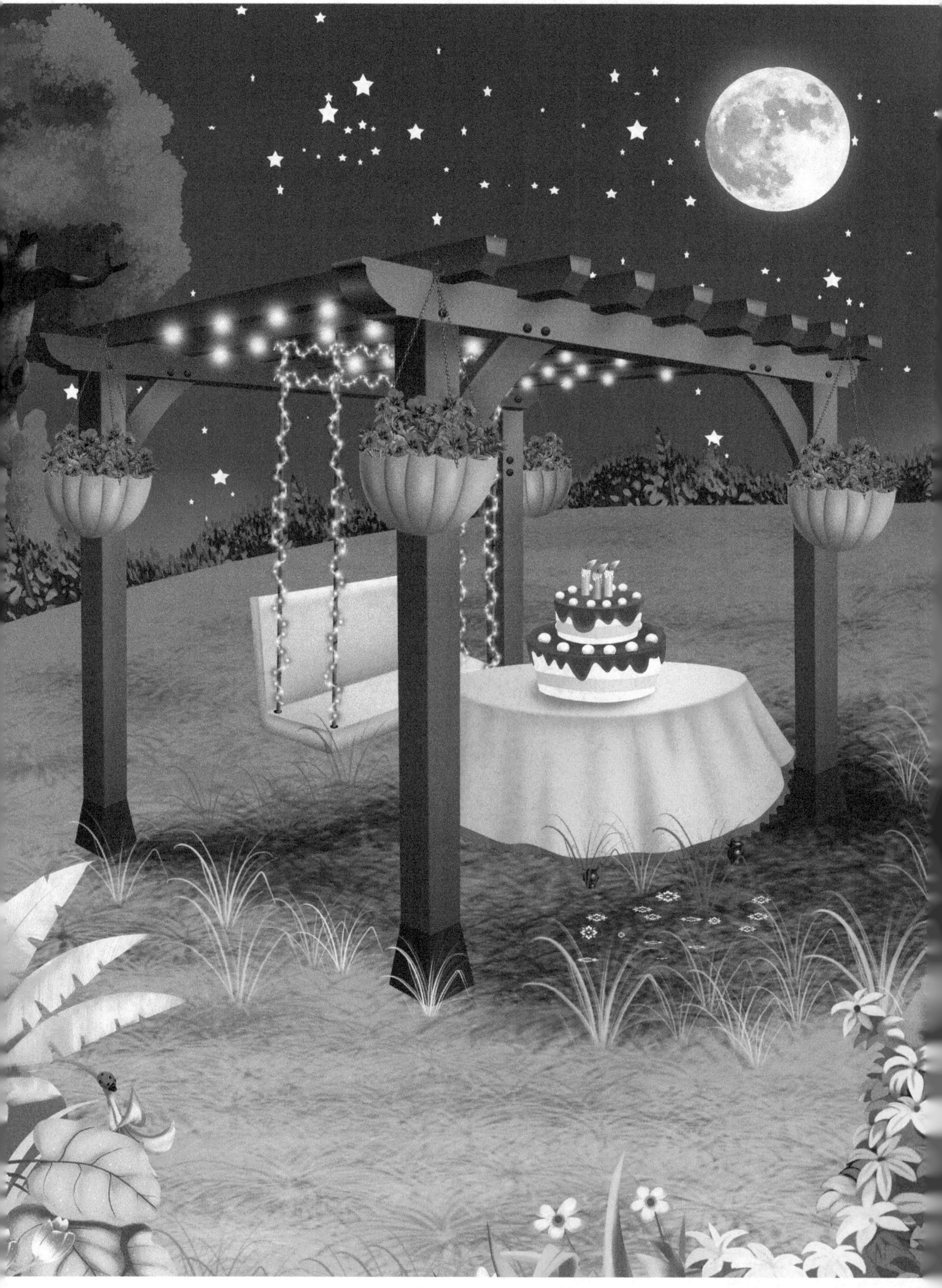

Sarayu and Kautilya's face beamed with happiness. Their eyes

shone like jewels on a queen's crown. They stepped outside. The pergola and swing stood firm under the clear blue sky, dazzling with lights and hanging flowerpots, just like the kids' visioned.

In front of the swing was a cake, with the letters HAPPY BIRTHDAY gleaming.

"Happy birthday sweethearts!", the parents wished them.

"We are happy with the way you guys patiently waited to get on the swing that you dreamed for months. You did not get upset or angry. Patience is a virtue!"

At last, Sarayu and Kautilya got to sit on their favorite swing.

It was a day they will cherish forever.

Grandma's Talking Garden

Grandma's vegetable garden had a high reputation in the village. She grew all kinds of organic vegetables like cabbage, cauliflower, lettuce, eggplants, bitter gourd, bottle gourd, chillies, cilantro etc. Grandma has a son who lived with his family in a city nearby. They visited her once every month. The grandkids especially loved visiting her because they get to play with neighbor children.

Grandma's love reflected in her cooking. She prepared food with vegetables hand-picked from her garden.

"Grandma! We're here!", the kids shouted from the lowered windows of their car even before they got down.

The old lady welcomed them. It was lunchtime.

"Grandma, what's special for lunch today?"

"I made eggplant-cilantro curry, boiled veggies topped with salt and pepper, sambar and lemon rice for you dearies," grandma beamed as she read the menu.

The kids frowned. "Vegetables again! We hate vegetables! Anyway, please serve us quick grandma, we want to go out and play with neighbor kids,"

"Oh no! They are at their grandparents' place. I believe

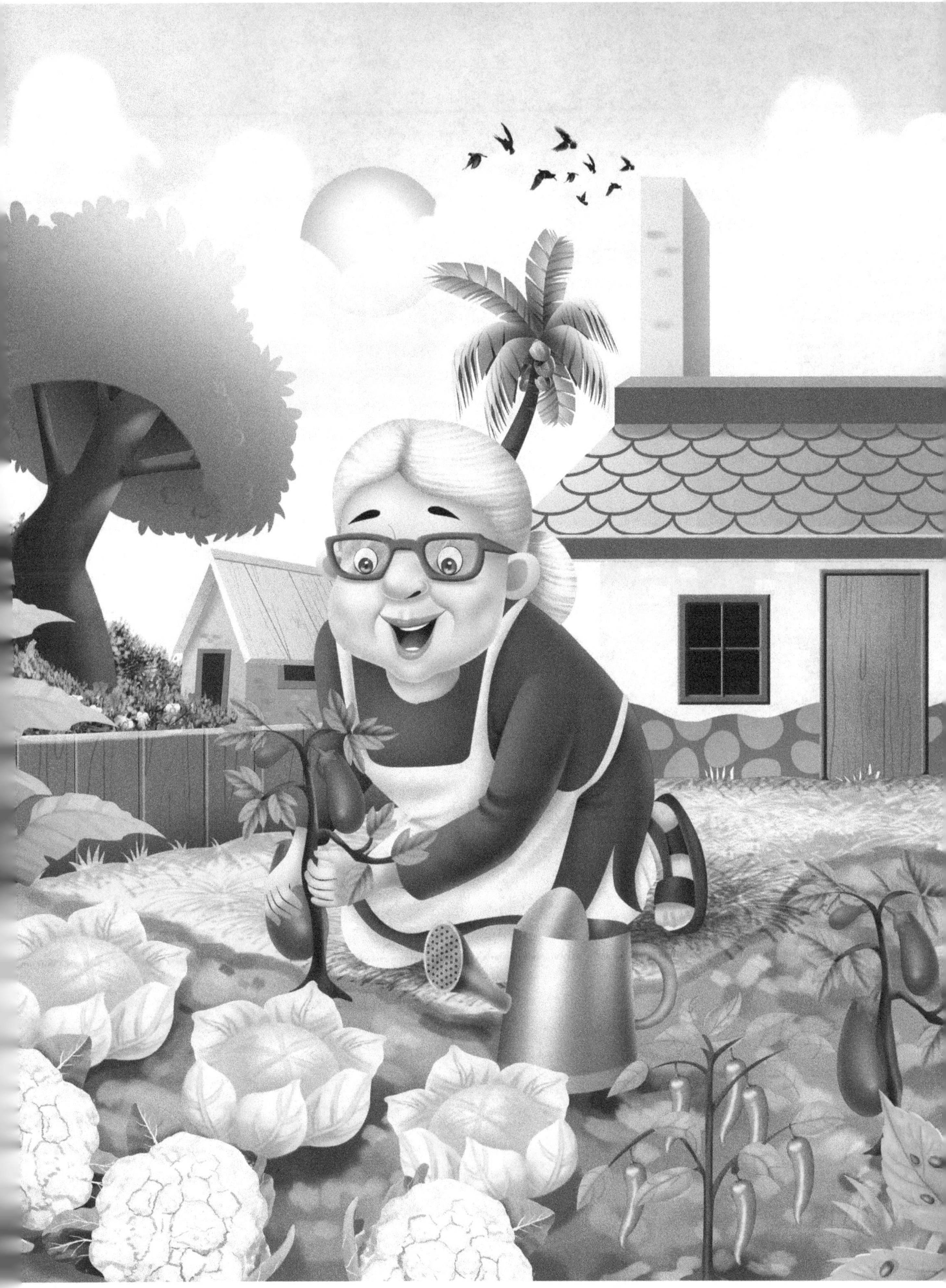

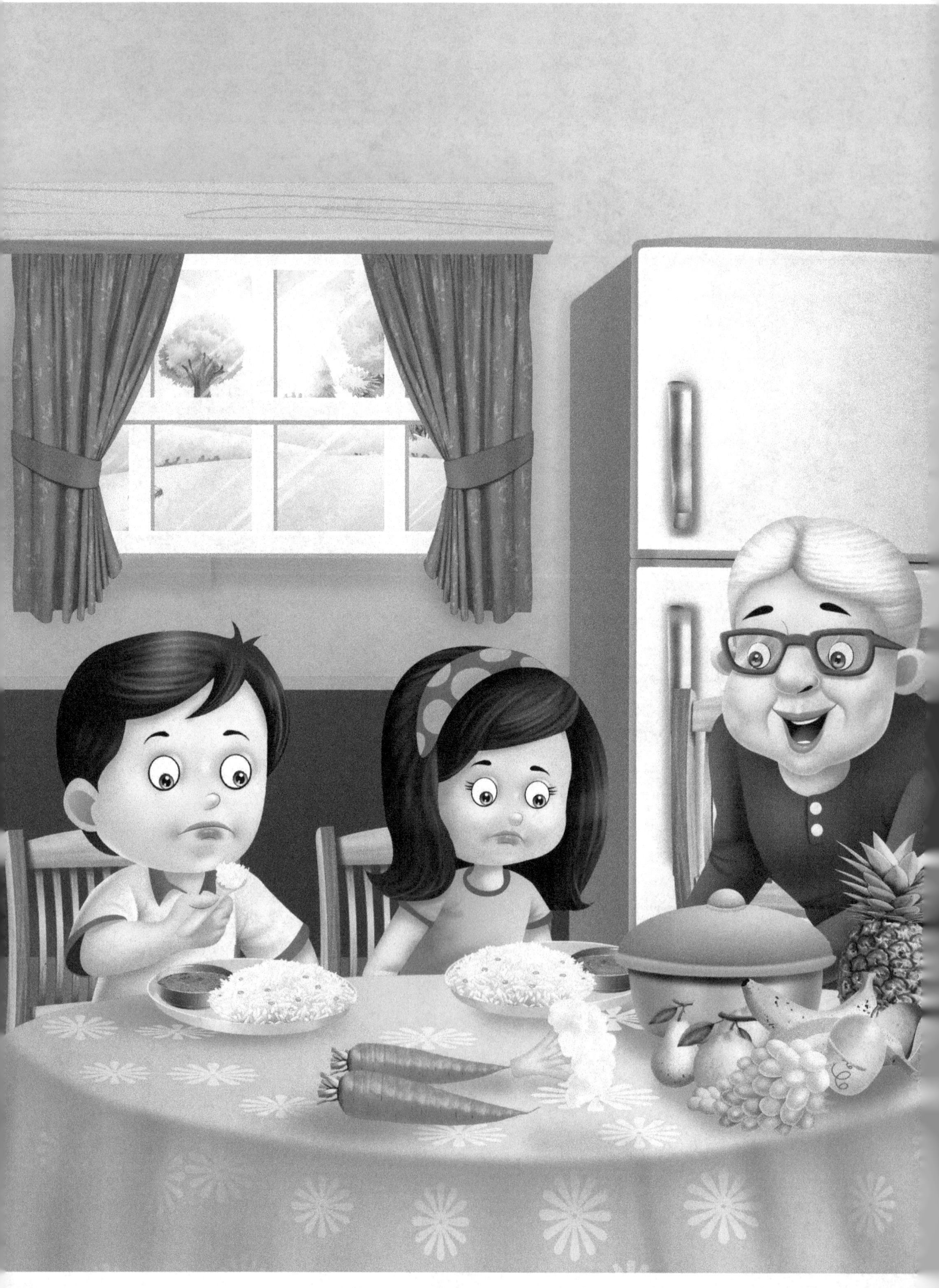

they won't be back until next month," saying so Grandma read the disappointment on the kids' faces. She continued, "You know how famous my garden is in this village, right? For a change, learn about the efforts I put behind it."

The kids accepted reluctantly. They had nothing better to do.

Next morning, the kids were woken up early. Mornings are usually best time to water plants because it allows water to reach the roots without getting evaporated due to heat.

"Children, this is green chilli plant. There are more chillies than you see. Most of them camouflage with leaves, thus misleading us. It is fun finding them. Come on, begin plucking!"

The uninterested children did as grandma directed. As they began plucking, they heard a noise.

"Psst......"

They looked up. There was no one. Grandma was busy watering the plants at a distance. Ignoring the noise, they got back to work. They heard it again!

This time, it was loud and clear. It was coming from the chilli plant!

The duo was in for a shock. Upon observing clearly, they noticed that it was coming from a tiny little green chilli hiding behind a leaf.

"Are you trying to talk to us?", the kids asked.

"Yes!"

"Oh god! You can actually talk!", the kids exclaimed.

"It's not just me! All my friends here can talk," she said, pointing her tail towards other vegetables in the garden.

Leafy the cabbage and Flory the cauliflower waved at the kids.

Beaming with delight, the kids asked, "Do you talk to grandma too?"

"No!"

"Then why us?"

"Because you children think we are boring. Do you realize how valuable our vegetable family is? We nourish you; we help you grow. We provide all that you need for a healthy living. We eagerly wait for the opportunity to get inside you and help you develop. But children like you ignore us! Do you know my friend Leafy is an excellent source of vitamin C? Flory over there is rich in fiber and antioxidants. What more, my friends spinach, carrot and broccoli are

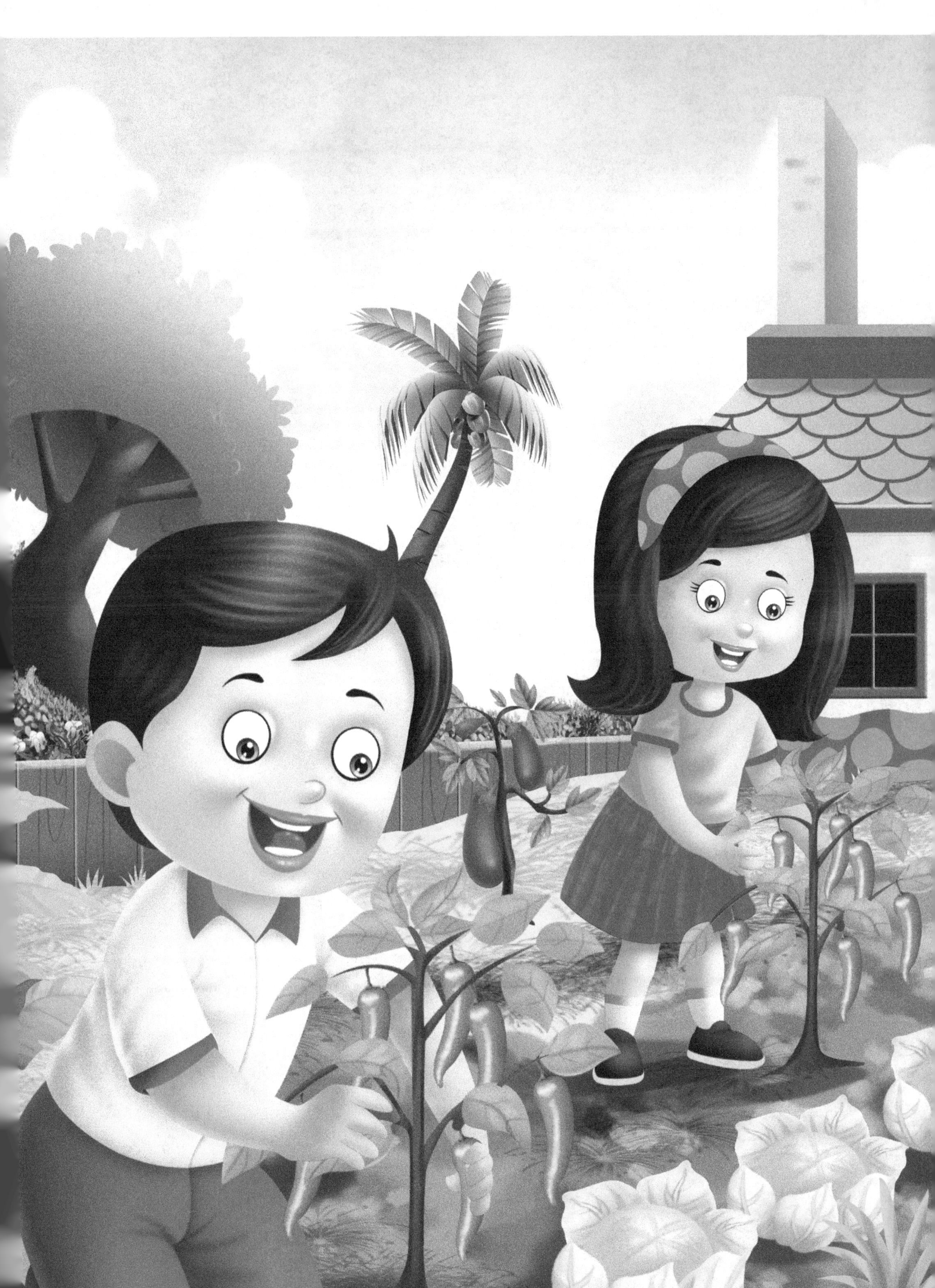

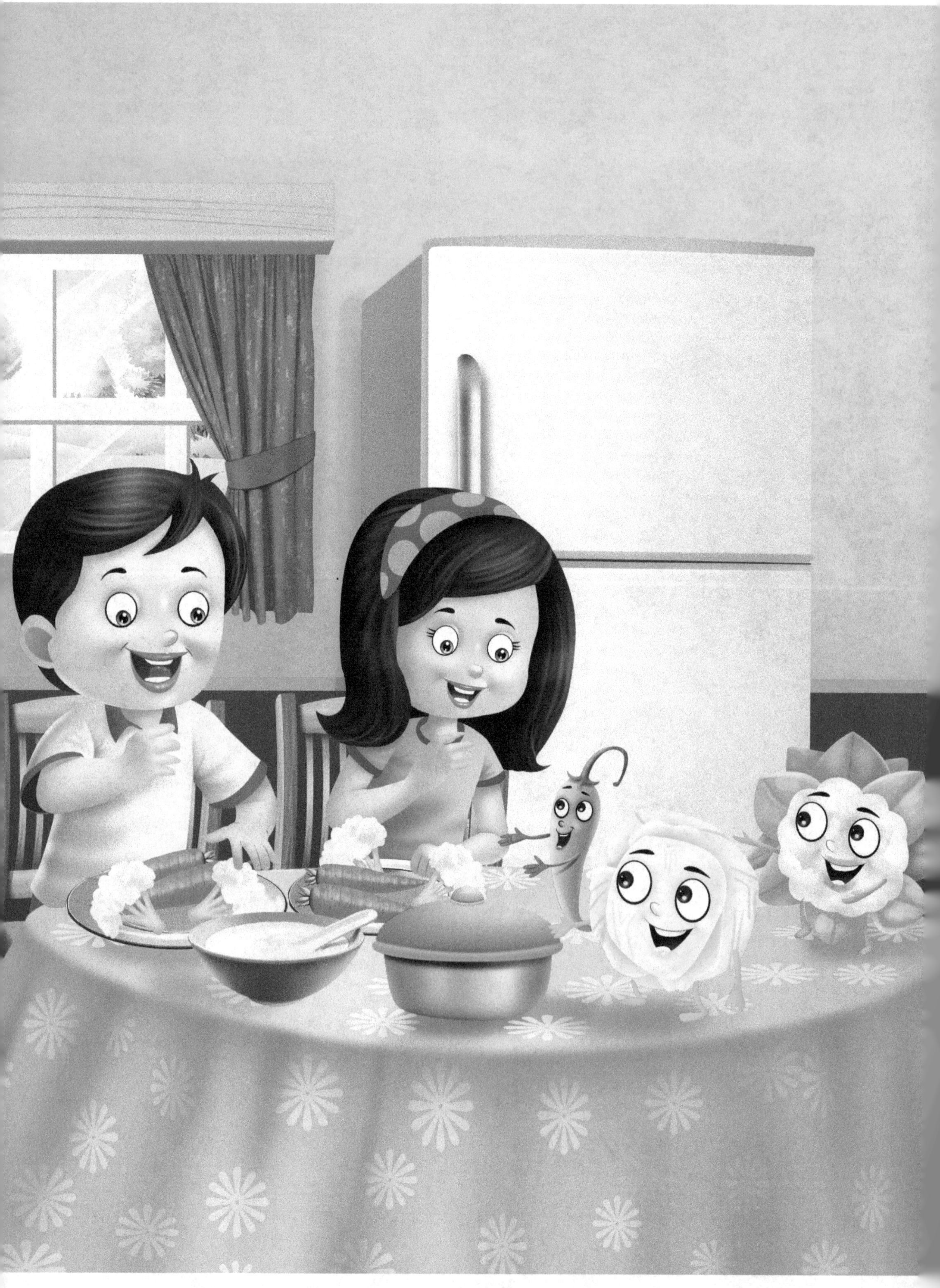

among the 14 healthiest vegetables on earth. We are sad that you do not give us enough importance," concluded chilli with a sad face. The kids realized the importance of their vegetable portions.

"We have always ignored our portion of veggies. We promise we will never repeat this mistake. You take care of us well! Sorry for realizing your value this late."

Grandma appeared from behind, "Who are you talking to?"

"No one grandma! Working here, we realized how valuable vegetables are and all the good they do for us. We promise to never neglect our vegetables again,"

Grandma was puzzled by the kids' confession but was happy with the change her efforts brought in them.

Srivalli's Pen Friend

Srivalli was bored. No activity could keep her engaged for more than an hour. It was peak summer in India. The scorching heat prevented her from playing with her friends outdoors. Indoor games were not Srivalli's cup of tea.

She looked for ways to keep herself engaged, but in vain. She read books, helped her mother in cooking and doing dishes, watched TV etc. No matter what she did, she still had ample time left.

Srivalli's mother noticed her daughter's restlessness. She came up with an idea.

"Srivalli, why don't you write to a pen pal?"

"A pen pal? I don't understand what you are talking about, mom!"

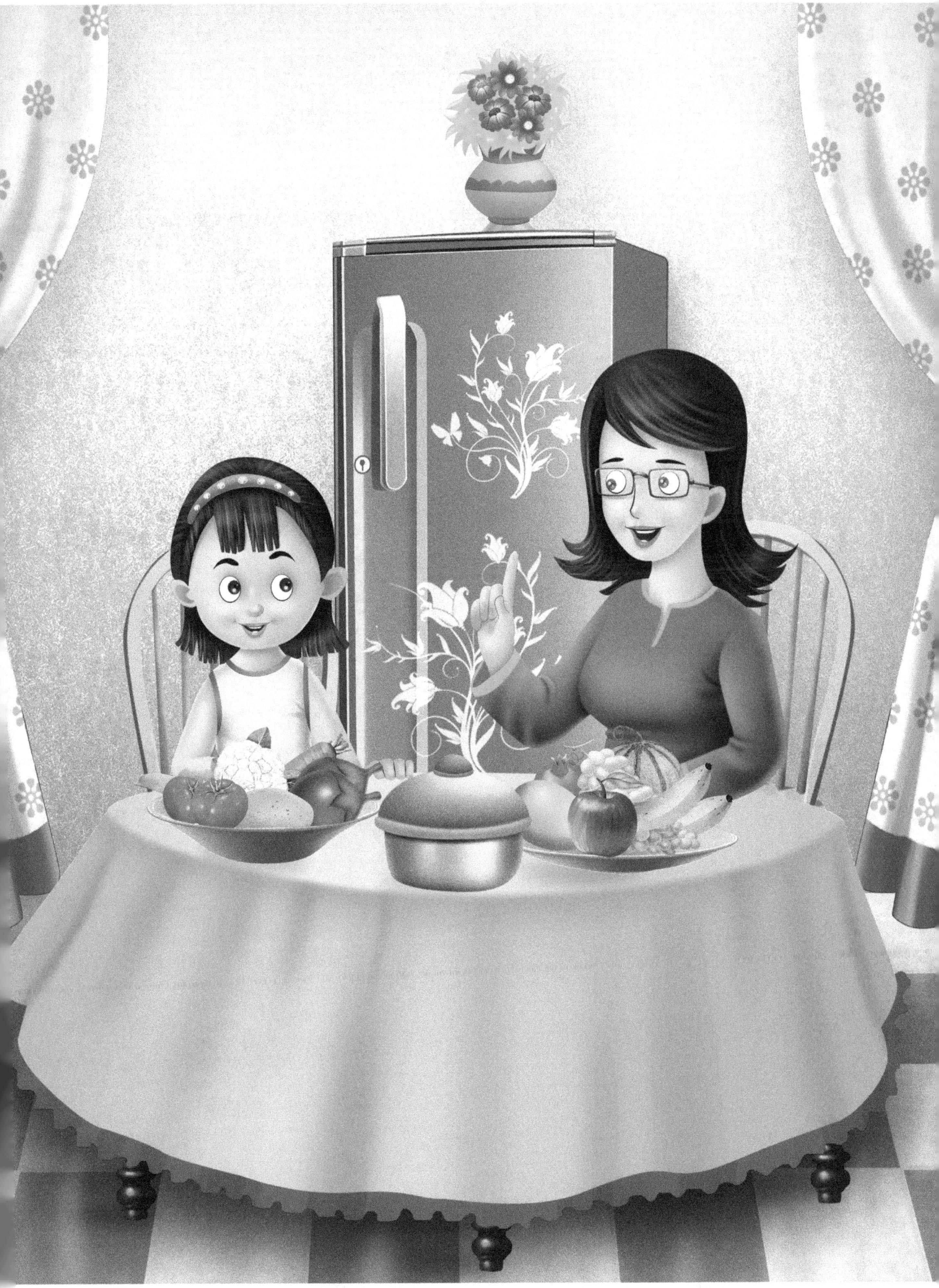

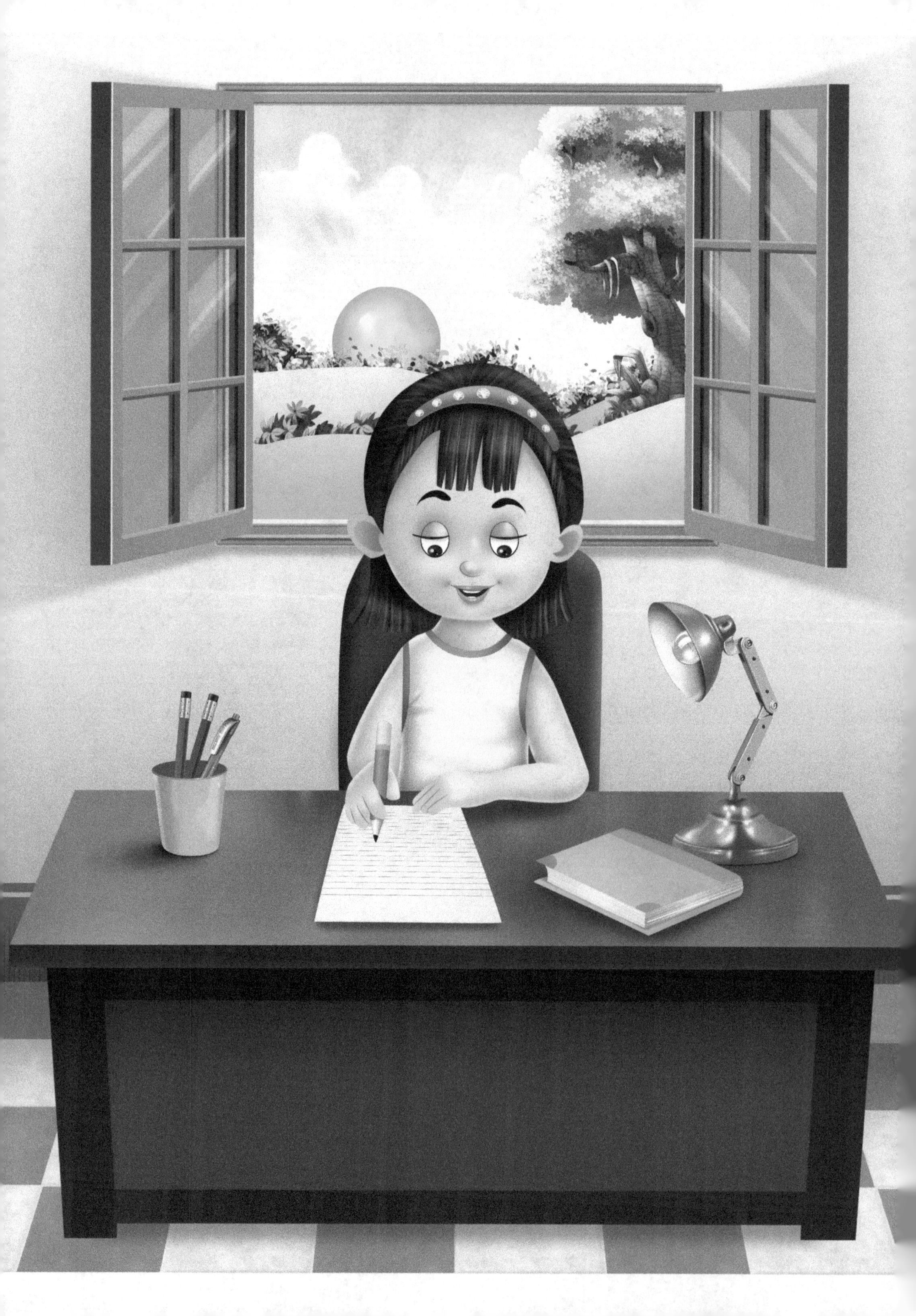

"Pen pals are usually strangers that you have never met. Your friendship solely depends on exchange of letters."

"Where do they live, mom?"

"They could be right across the street or up in the arctic circle! You never know."

"But mom, isn't social media also about making friends with strangers? Why should I bother writing to someone when I know I can make friends online and receive quick responses? What is so special about pen friendship?"

"I agree social media has brought strangers together. But, the beauty of pen friendship is unique. Pen pals are never judgmental. Just imagine that you are writing to someone. You pour your heart on the paper. You send it to them and wait for them to write back. There is a magical feeling in the wait. It is always worth it. Besides, it teaches you to be patient while waiting for the person's response.

Trust me, pen pals are for lifelong."

"Really?"

"Suppose you get a message on your phone. At the same time, you get a handwritten letter from someone. Which one will you open first?"

"The letter, of course! Handwritten letters are rare in this texting era. I would love to read something addressed solely to me."

"There you go!"

"But mom, how do I find a pen friend?"

"You can use internet for this, Srivalli. There are a couple of websites that help you find pen pals. Find someone. I am glad you are doing this. All the best!"

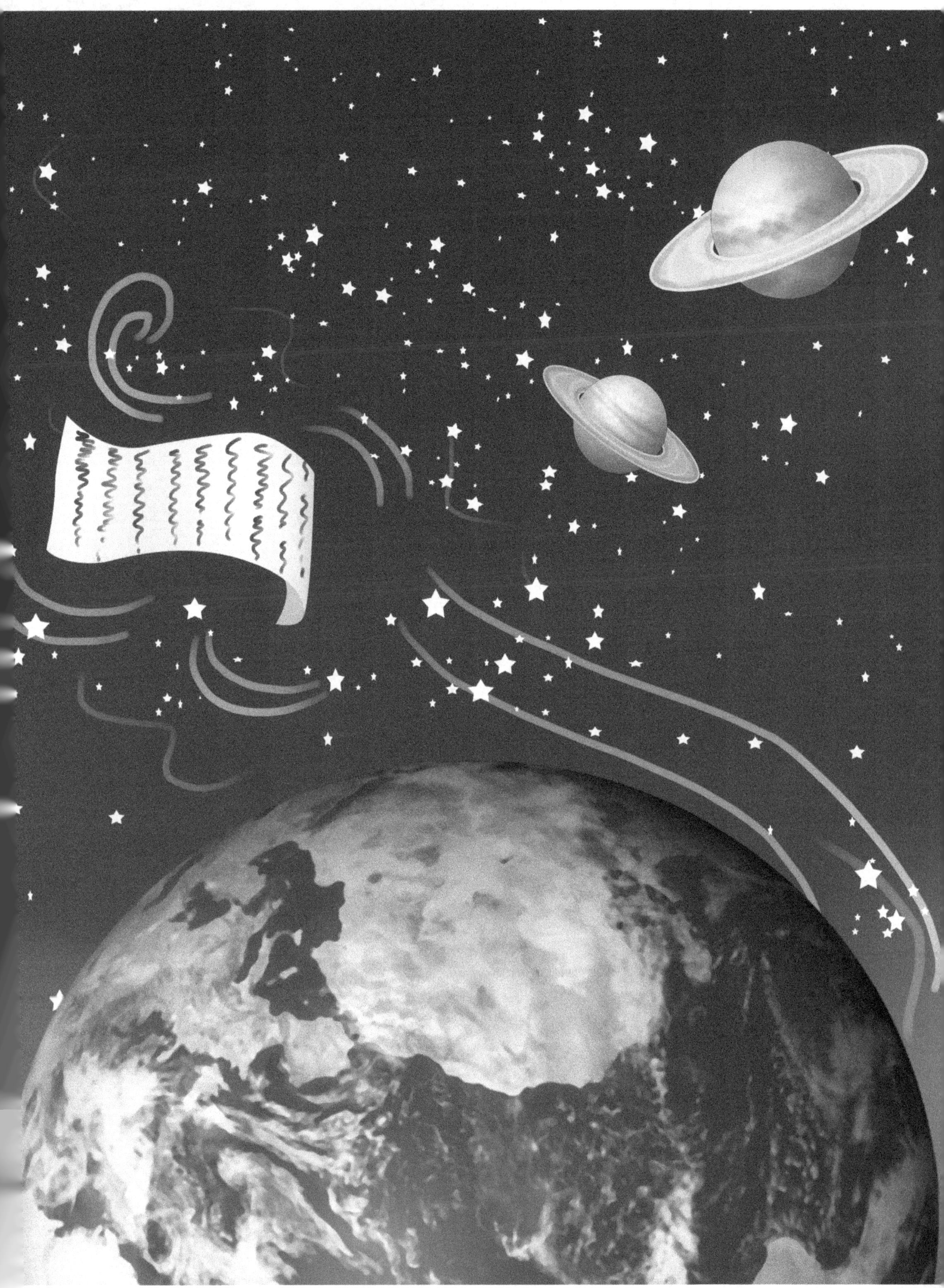

Srivalli was super excited. She went online and found a pen pal who lives in Oklahoma. Two weeks after she sent her first letter, Srivalli got a letter addressed to her.

Srivalli's mother was happy that she was finally able to get her daughter engaged in something that would last lifetime.

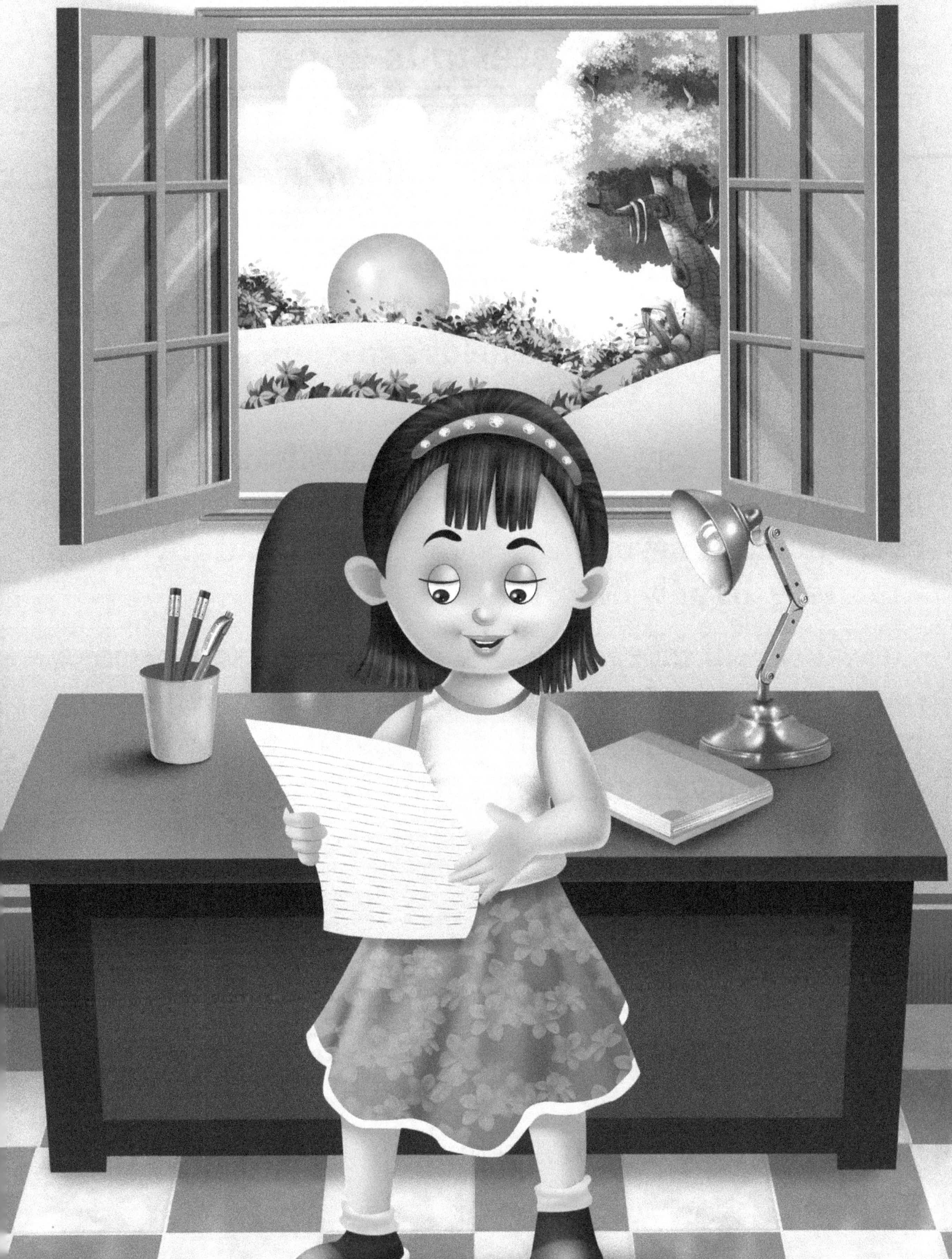

The Mysterious Cookie

Craig and Dan were best friends. They lived in neighboring houses far away from city-lights. Their houses were surrounded by corn fields on all sides. A small snake-like muddy road between the two houses made its way through the fields and connected to the main road.

Dan suffered from childhood asthma. His parents never let him play outdoor games because they feared it might cause him trouble breathing. Dan hardly had any friends. Craig was his only best friend.

The duo spent most summer afternoons reading books, narrating stories to each other and painting. When bored, they lay on the bed and stared at the cornfields and speeding vehicles on main road. Craig loved Dan's company more than anyone.

One night, Craig finished his dinner and sat by the little window of his bedroom. The sky was clear. He had never seen so many stars in the sky. Excited, Craig started counting them.

After counting more than a hundred stars, he lost track.

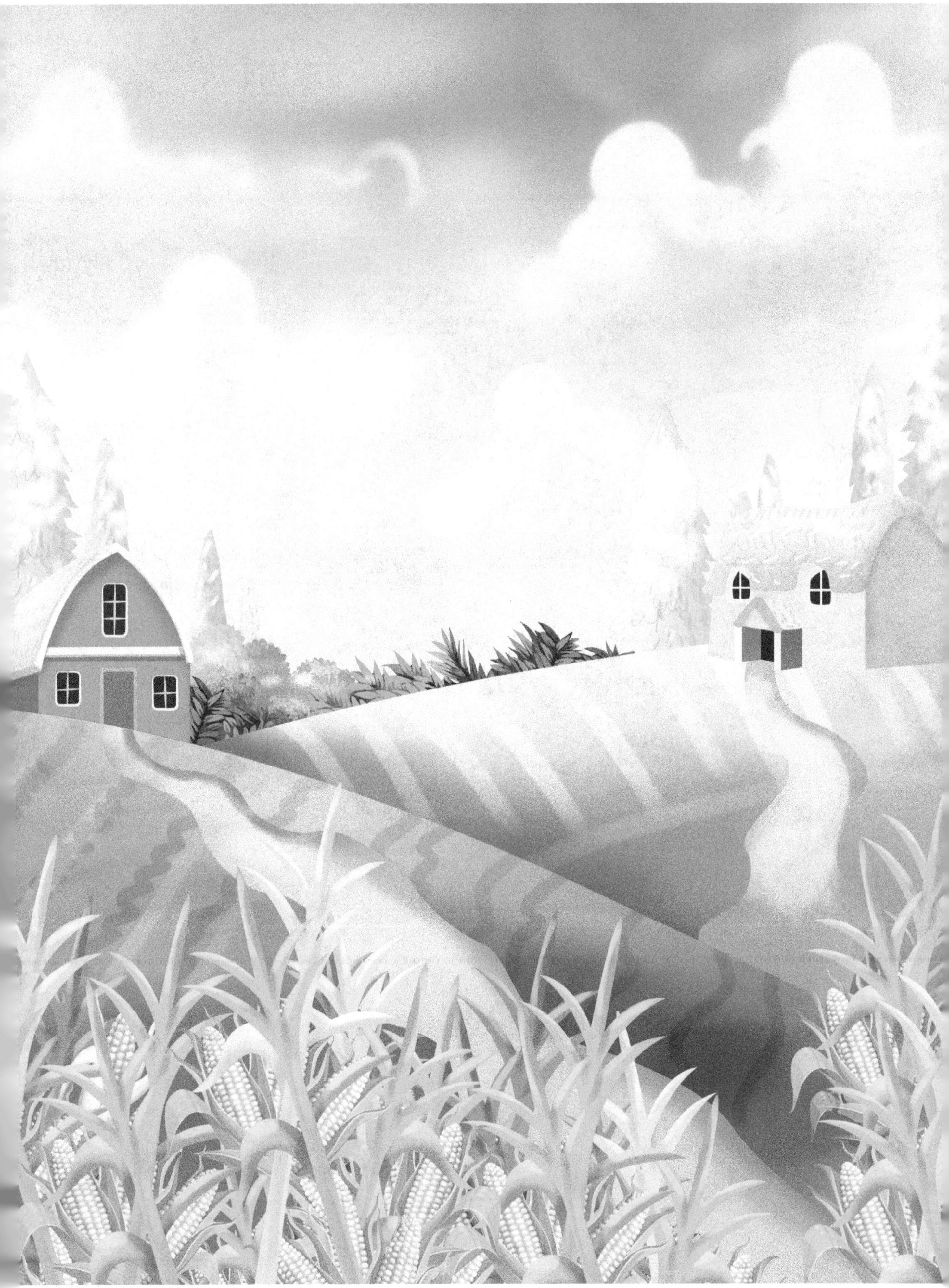

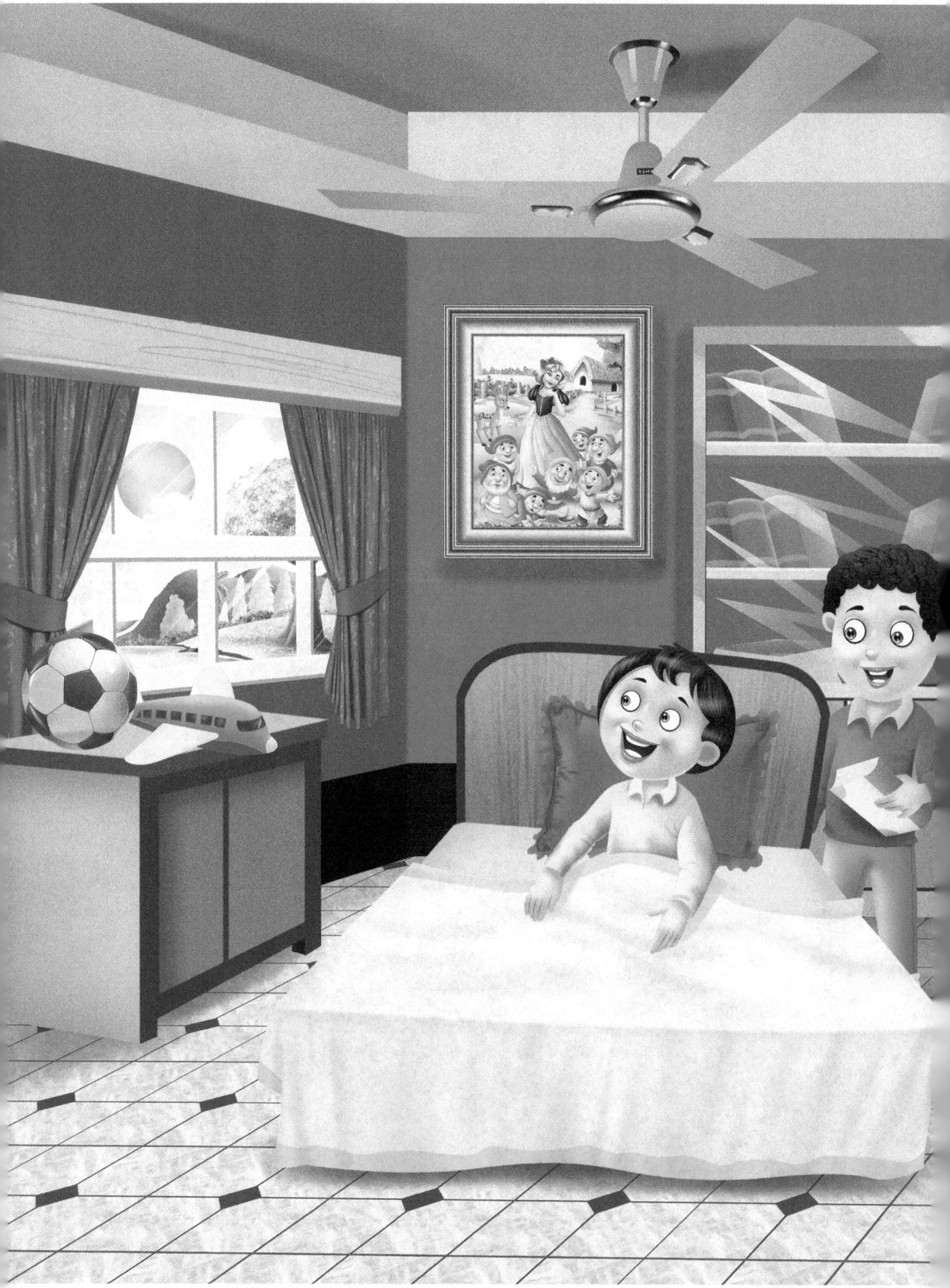

Confused and irritated, Craig looked down. He noticed an old man on the road. Though he could not figure out who it was, Craig was sure that it was not anybody from his or Dan's family. The lights went off and everyone was asleep.

As the old man neared, Craig shouted from his window, "Who are you?"

"I am a homeless old man. Could you please give me some water to drink?" the old man replied.

Craig hesitated for a second. It was late at night and everyone was fast asleep. He did not want to be in trouble, but the old man seemed genuine.

"Please wait," he said and fetched a glass of water. Craig handed over the glass of water from his bedroom window.

"God bless you, my child. You helped me in need. As a parting gift, I would love to reward you with something valuable I have," saying so the old man pulled out a cookie from his ragged bag.

"What is this? I am sorry, but I am not supposed to accept food from strangers," Craig blurted.

"Well, that's a good habit, son. But this is not an edible cookie. This is a magic cookie. Whosoever possesses this never gets sick and becomes the strongest person ever!

But remember, you should keep it with you. If you give it away to anyone, it will stop working for you even if you get it back from them," the old man explained.

Craig was excited. The strongest person ever! "I must own this cookie," he thought.

" I rarely accept anything from strangers, but you look genuine.

I will take the cookie," he said.

The old man smiled and handed it over.

As soon as Craig thanked him, the man waved and vanished into thin air. Just like that!

Craig was shocked. He could not believe what he saw. "This man and his cookie must definitely be magical!", he thought.

The next morning, Craig noticed that his family was re-arranging living room. He helped his mother lift and move a heavy wooden chair in the living room. He effortlessly moved the TV and TV table. Everyone was taken by surprise at his display of strength. No one knew the secret except for Craig.

Smiling, he knocked on Dan's door to narrate the previous night's events. Dan opened the door, coughing. He looked sad.

"What happened Dan?"

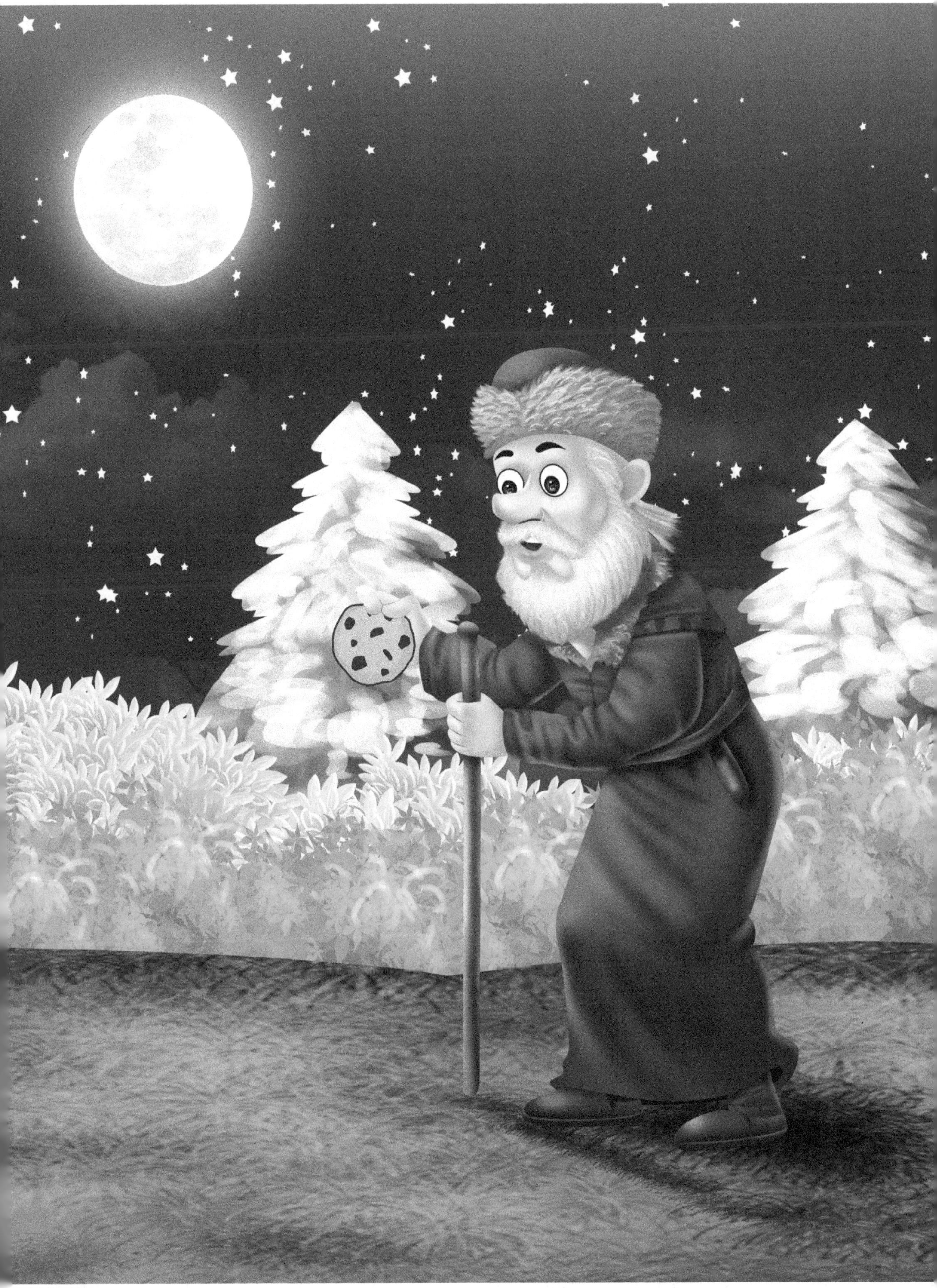

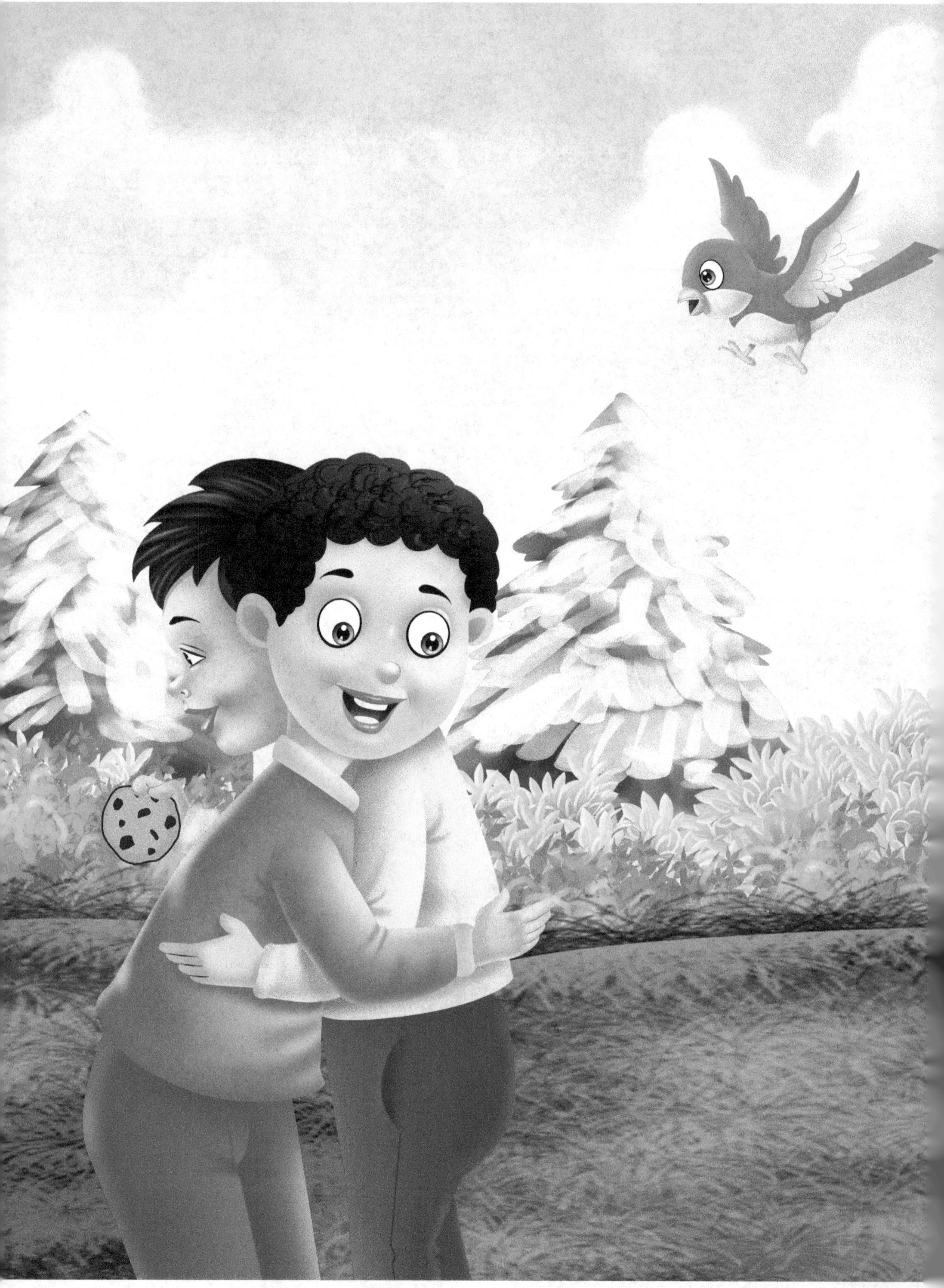

"I was playing football in our backyard. Suddenly, I started coughing and could not breathe. Mom and dad came to my rescue. They scolded me for running. Sometimes, it is hard to digest the fact that this is how my life is going to be"

Craig paused for a moment and smiled. His face beamed with delight. He asked Dan to follow him to the latter's bedroom.

"What is it, Craig?"

"I have something for you. But promise me, you are going to keep it with you forever,"

"Sure! But what is it?"

Craig narrated what happened previous night.

"But Craig! This belongs to you. I don't want to take it away from you!"

"Listen to me, Dan. I did have the urge in me to keep it. After all, who wouldn't want to be the strongest person ever? But a voice in my head told me that not everything you desire needs to be yours. If I keep it, it will only be an added advantage. There is nothing I lose if I part with this magical cookie. For you, it will open the doors to a whole new world that you thought you could explore only in your wildest dreams!"

Dan was still not convinced. He felt it is selfish to accept something that his friend earned. He was about to say no when Craig slipped the cookie into his pocket!

Dan stood still, shocked. Craig's move was totally unexpected.

"Why did you do it Craig?," Dan's voice quivered as he asked.

Craig did not speak a word. Instead, he hugged Dan tight. That moment, their hearts exchanged millions of unspoken words of love.

From that day on, Dan and Craig played a lot of outdoor games in Dan's backyard and no one ever yelled at them.

CPSIA information can be obtained
at www.ICGtesting.com
Printed in the USA
BVHW061054230621
610291BV00003B/328